The Home Run Crew
"Learning the Game with Confidence

by: TARNESHIA S. WILLIAMS

Inspired by: Cash Williams

2

The Home Run Crew "Learning the Game with Confidence

by: TARNESHIA S. WILLIAMS

Inspired by: Cash Williams

Dedication

"To every kid who's ever
picked up a bat and
BELIEVED

It was the first day of baseball season. The sun was out, the grass was freshly cut, and Cash was already at the field—cap pulled low, glove in hand. "Captain Cash reporting for duty," he said with a grin. Dylan showed up next, quiet but focused. "Let's just not drop any balls today." Then came Carson—running, nearly tripping over his bat. "Did we start yet? Did I miss anything?!"

Coach Mordy clapped his hands. "Welcome to the team, boys! This season isn't about being perfect. It's about learning the game, working hard, and playing with confidence." Cash nodded like a leader. Dylan gave a thumbs up. Carson jumped into the air yelling, "Let's play ball!"

Practice wasn't easy. Cash hesitated when the team asked him what to do next. "Uh... just... do your best?" he said, unsure.Dylan missed two grounders in a row and looked down at his shoes.Carson struck out during hitting drills and tossed his helmet off. "Ugh! I'll never hit anything!"

Coach pulled them aside. "Mistakes mean you're learning. Confidence isn't something you start with—it's something you build."Cash looked at his teammates. "Okay... let's help each other out."Dylan smiled. "Yeah. We've got this."Carson gave a thumbs up. "Let's keep swinging!"

The team started doing drills. Cash helped Carson line up his stance. Dylan practiced catching pop flies with Coach. "That's it, Carson. Keep your eyes on the ball," said Cash. "Nice grab, Dylan!" yelled Coach. Carson swung and hit the ball. It wasn't far, but he beamed. "I hit it! I really hit it!"

They practiced every day after school. Cash got better at leading, Dylan started trusting his hands, and Carson stopped worrying about striking out. "Let's go, team!" Cash would say. "We've got this," Dylan echoed. "Best team ever!" Carson added, always with a jump.

17

Game day arrived. The bleachers were packed. Cash took a deep breath. "Okay team… just play like we practiced."Dylan looked serious. "No dropped balls."Carson whispered, "Please let me hit something."

The game was close. Cash made smart calls. Dylan caught a tough pop fly. Carson hit the ball and made it to first base. "Yes!" he cheered. Coach shouted from the dugout, "That's what I'm talking about, team!"

In the final inning, the score was tied. Cash stepped up to the plate. He looked at Dylan and Carson, then at the pitcher. "Let's end this strong," he thought. He swung— CRACK! The ball soared to center field. "Run!" Coach shouted.

Cash ran to first. Dylan was on third and dashed home. Carson clapped and yelled, "We're doing it!"The crowd roared as Dylan slid into home. SAFE!They had won the game.The team jumped and shouted, piling into a group hug.

After the game, Coach gathered the team. "You didn't just win—you worked hard, helped each other, and stayed confident."Cash looked around. "We make a great team." Dylan nodded. "Even when we mess up."Carson threw his arms up. "Let's play forever!"

From that day on, they weren't just players. They were the Home Run Crew—confident, caring, and ready for anything.Because learning baseball was just the beginning.

THE END

"Inspired by my own family's love for baseball…"

Thanks for Reading!"

Thank you for reading The Home Run Crew!
Keep swinging, keep smiling, and always believe in yourself.

⚾ More adventures coming soon!

Draw Your Own Team!"

⚾ Activity Page:

Draw yourself and your dream baseball team below!

Draw Your Own Team!"

Made in the USA
Monee, IL
14 August 2025

23283409R10021